Painting Over Sketches of Anatolia

ver design by Doowah Design.
oto of Leonard Neufeldt by Michael Elwell.

is book was printed on Ancient Forest Friendly paper.
nted and bound in Canada by Hignell Book Printing Inc.

gratitude to editors of the following publications, in which some
these poems appeared, several in earlier versions: *The Barnwood
view, Canadian Literature, Contemporary Verse 2, December,
ent, Half in the Sun* (anthology), *Literary Review of Canada, The
w Quarterly, Poems From Planet Earth* (anthology), *Portland
view, Prairie Fire, Prism International, Queen's Quarterly, Rhubarb,
d Sycamore Review.* Several of the Turkish poems appeared as a
apbook titled *How to Beat the Heat in Bodrum.*

acknowledge the support of The Canada Council for the Arts and
Manitoba Arts Council for our publishing program.

brary and Archives Canada Cataloguing in Publication

ufeldt, Leonard, 1937-, author
Painting over sketches of Anatolia / Leonard Neufeldt.

ems.
3N 978-1-927426-65-4 (pbk.)

I. Title.

8577.E758P35 2015 C811'.54 C2015-901415-8

gnature Editions
). Box 206, RPO Corydon, Winnipeg, Manitoba, R3M 3S7
vw.signature-editions.com

PAINTING OVER SKETCH OF ANATOLIA

LEONARD NEUFELDT

George Payerle, Editor

Signature
EDITIONS

For Larry Buell and Jupp Schöpp,
with a friend's embrace,

and, as always,
for Mera

Contents

Portraits in Different Voices

Painting Over Sketches of Anatolia

Think of This Earth, My Love

PORTRAITS IN DIFFERENT VOICES

The End of Plato

Either the wind or some animal's
distress. Even if one knew,
what difference would it make except to remind you
that too much knowing is earthbound,
that winter has come to live with you like a son
newly divorced, his life spread out in every room?
Numbness buoys you, but you still feel
the anger. It's here, you tell yourself,
relief from the damn night, although
you always chose your words more carefully
in your writings and with students,
'a style sweet as honey on the lips,' they said,
'like Solon's lyrical verse but more eloquent,'
and less edgy than Socrates, the voices
rinsed free of bitterness like grape leaves
picked in the morning for the evening meal.
Nonetheless, no matter how innocent,
how slight, your errors may just ruin
everything you meant

Strips of clouds hang heavy between
the window shutters open as always,
and you hear the rain begin with an equilibrium
of soft sound. When the night maid leaves
and the young man arrives for the usual dictation,
he will bring more food and wine
and stronger medication for sleep,
and he will ask again whether there is feeling
on the right side. Because he loves his ways
more than wisdom you will try to explain
yet again that any feeling on any side is for
the unfinished Dialogue, and you will search
for words he understands. Your voice

will be Socrates' asking if what is real
in a poem or politics or the wind-harp's wild hum
comes from this world moving in on all sides,
flush with feeling, comfortless
as your good side

That is what you fear
more than dying

Margaret Fuller Returns to New York

There is evidence that while the Elizabeth was breaking up [upon the rocks of Fire Island on July 19, 1850, Fuller] could have been rescued, had she wanted to exert herself. Within sight of America, Margaret Fuller chose to perish with her husband and her child.

— Perry Miller

Separateness washing under you as if to draw
you back into the surf, denying your silence
but finding it again, more quickly this time

the eddies more certain. Amid these bargains
you hold still, and when the sea finally shakes off
the full length of your body, leaving crystals

in the dark of your eyes and in lines
below your chin, you are heavier in the face,
neck, midriff than when Greeley saw you off

at the pier's first-class gate four years ago —
Europe will be yours, but don't forget
your friends and your nation. Write often

On your side, you stare into an ocean's
weariness, right arm outstretched, the wind
unforgiving as revolutions and people

without hope. You will want to find your hands,
wipe flecks of sand from your face, grow
thoughtful, surprised that terror is limited

to remembering someone in front of you,
eyes half open, hair thrown forward,
lips white below a laser-blue of light, arms

holding nothing but themselves, you childless
again, no words at hand for any of this,
no longer fluent on the shore of the New World

After years abroad one must relearn usual speech

It's the same with drowning. This is the part
most difficult to explain to Greeley, Clarke,
and Emerson, who will want you to rewrite

your lost book, the book that brought you home
and of course you'll write it again, longer this time,
idioms less quaint, translations more exact

beginnings not what they were, wars remembered
differently, ends vanished under waves like
children, sometimes things impossible to imagine

already there. And when it's finally done
and you give it not to them but page by page to the sea,
you'll have to go even farther away than this

Auguste Rodin

Morning annealed like stone hammered
with the night's anger into thoughtfulness

But the two memorials next week
my neighbour's and a friend in Berlin

A friend's death can change the past
entirely. I'll travel alone

and someone will take it personally
someone will ask which side I'm on

as though everything comes down to that
to the fault-finding between us

My eyes and hands hold their own disputes
fully formed for days at a time

over all the images sleep has smashed
before the morning can shake them off

like too much thinking, too much loss
and crouch forward toward its fate

Röcken, Germany: Nietzsche Grave and Monument

Joseph's knee bends past its misery
to the simple lid of your grave beside your father's
to place our golden gerberas above and below
your name. "You, the ultimate Protestant, buried
our past," he says with the faraway voice of a Jesuit
drop-out. "It's more than the classics and the Church
and much more than a lover's quarrels
but that's how it begins." Perhaps he means
a future almost ready for the mind's hazards
and the word's chaos of joy turning the present over
and over like astonishment, like the passion
of the new will to be both prophet and poet.
Our wives watching, a way of taking sides,
the moment balanced on the shining edge of wonder
sharp with doubt. Prussian citizenship
and the old grammar of suffering and charity
bargained away for pure voice, for the
satyr in our sentences, for pitiless
sayings insistent as a trumpeter

Your father's church austere as the symmetry
of the two graves below the two windows
of the south wall, the slant of light articulate

In front of the church an angular island of shade.
Trees find fault with slightest wind
where you stand straight-backed with your mother
and confidants, all of you
surprised by chalk-whiteness, but only you
ready for another life, you alone
naked, about to explain everything,
Joseph and I finding this dream believable
as your books' poor sales back then,

only forty copies of the fourth part of *Zarathustra*
printed. How would they ever know that God
is dead, that even with our help his death
was natural, that he knew the truth before
he died? That the book of saints and Attic heroes
was returned long ago with all its damage?
Your dream impatient enough
to cover more of you and move the hat
that's over your genitals
back to your head, your right hand free
to explain how madness divines impossibilities
of nations warmed by glorias as cold
as dead stars, whatever replaces them,
whatever name for it, argued in aphorisms
that sometimes leap at us, sometimes snuff out
like torches in the wind, sometimes luring
and holding us until denial gasps
like lungs emptied

                                        and you felt a tiredness
you never knew existed. That's how it is
with prophets, Joseph would say, so much belief,
so much unbelief, so much madness, the times heady,
remorseless as spirochetes that never sleep.
If only your father's homilies had said
at least half as much. If only your mother
had tried to understand what you had said
about the dream, its new formalities

Pierre Loti

Evening. The enflamed breath of the Bosporus borne
narrowly along, the spine's memory-board alive

After we picked white mulberries the women
shook out dark hair; small leaves and stems
fell to the ground like olives, but without the olives'
sound. And when we weeded the narrowness
of our friend Eva's mounded grave, the day's knowing
headed home like the sky's calligraphy

Pierre Loti, your usual table and usual chair
high above the waters of the Golden Horn
were comfortable, the vast burial slope of the poor
and the turbaned great just below, tea
and raki glasses almost empty,
your journal notebook almost full.
You were right, no doubt: most words not learned
of love or woe are soon forgotten. But had you not
been fitted for a new name,
would the distance between your journal entries
and romance have remained the same,
a mere water-taxi crossing, Europe
to Asia or back? Gulls of the Bosporus
screaming behind you,
a city's minarets floating free

Trotsky Explains Lenin to Frida Kahlo

He wore deep learning as disguise,
believable, perfect cover
for that love of self that burns with a low blue
fire you can hold in an open hand,
but dare not, the miracle
deferred for the flame's fuel,
and the mystery of how
it sets itself ablaze, burns steadfast
as sulfur in a swamp or a people's
revolution, the memory
its small shapes spark
long afterward in those
who like to bring past and future round
to anthems of praise, every word
sweeping its heat skyward,
burning the night air black
to its very edge, words
I passed my hands through,
hurting them

because Stalin
had invented fire so cold
it can reach all the way back
to Nothing, beyond the last
frozen sleeve of stars

Earle Birney

I've come to surround my pauses with space.
— Earle Birney, *Selected Poems, 1966*

What's left of the way is not to be denied,
a road that stops rather than push itself
over the edge and free-fall like a hawk's
shadow against the cliff. All but turning
back with nowhere else to go, a pause
that tells you you're on your own

The difference between pauses and space
clear as an alpine lake is the simplicity
of standing naked in the cold, waiting, a fire
started, fingers finding corners of two
blankets at the same time despite themselves
as you count icebergs near the far shore
where the glacier narrows the horizon to a wall

You have wrapped the blankets about you again,
breath pausing, each part of being here
surrounded by the water's clouded edge,
vaulted mountains and the wonder of time
as someone steps out the wide arc
between sun and cliff, starts the long way
down to the left, carefully, stops
for the back and forth of birds below and
for better footing, for the moment holding on

Baton with Tip Missing

Maestro Bernstein is teaching the dead to perform.
Being gone from the past is not to be freed of it,
but no *Messiah,* Prokofiev, Stern, Copeland
Gould. It's time to decide, he says at the end
of the break, whether orchestra and song and dance
can be beautiful on the sharp slope of after-
life without the innocence of new voices,
without their rag-and-bone hunger for balance
and uncertain desire, without the flea-
market politics of reviewers fretting
like nerves on the other side of endlessness

He auditions only those who worked with him
before, excluding those who needed to watch
the page and didn't look up, especially
brass players. Everyone rehearses
Candide and *West Side Story*
without a score, without his playing or singing
along, but his lips still mouth the music,
his left hand harrows wanton hair,
the ivory baton still reaches higher
than the highest note

And he's found a Maria.
Back there everyone said she looked
herself and that her last wish had been
for her surviving son to make a decent
living and not sleep the day away
and slouch forth into the sweet-sour
of night air like the long-backed rats
that had lost their fear of her. She says now
the only shoes she wears grip any surface,
and she may not suspect he chose her mainly
because of her range, how rapidly she learns

the music, how she follows his hands, which never stop
her, how she hits every note flawlessly
with or without accompaniment as if
she's always known her part, every detail,
although her body couldn't master desertion
and she can't imagine a famous conductor
with a damaged baton, the tip missing,
all the rehearsals in another room
without echoes, all the times
it was brought down hard

Fullness of Time

In her own time she could get hold
of things that go wrong,
and so having found her way
to the second stage
of Alzheimer's, she explained on a bridge
arching a small shudder of water
in Minter Gardens, where we
had taken her on a Sunday,
that ever since her husband had met
a bus head-on in northern Idaho
she didn't care for gardens,
and since her heart knew who she was
she couldn't begin to understand
her older sister's devotion to genealogy,
this zeal for missing elements.
"You can't change the past,"
not with a reading machine for macular
degeneration, not even with cataract surgery,
and her sister scheduled for both eyes,
her own eyes bright and furious
with unlearning, willing to let go
of bridge, stream, fountains, field of roses,
children, sisters all but one,
her gaze free of itself or tethered
to something far outside, beyond us,
beyond the great blue of Mount Cheam,
its glacier shadowed, inexact,
its bare peak bent by sky stretching
westward like a slope of light
called to praise by the evening bird

At night she leaves possibilities open,
window, birdless branch, eyes,
the soul, and a month ago

two nurses at the end of their day
found her five blocks away
in an intersection four lanes wide,
crosswalk zebra stripes gleaming white
between the idled cars
and horns quavering farther and farther back

the moon above her perfectly balanced,
and she at the centre, empty
summer purse turned double
in her fist, trying
without eyeglasses to remember
the way back out of the setting sun

Translating Paul Celan

Nothing is as it seems, but buds on the trellis are the colour
of wine. Crocus bowls brim with fresh snow

Not even the jay's scream of *I told you so* can reach
the hand's pressure on the open book beside the lamp

Learn to exchange advice for the words that stay near
the edge of the fear they escaped. Pigeon-dance of joy

Remember you're only a visitor; no word you unpack will be
the golem, no angel will step through the smoke far off

The second-longest poem has long since grown
used to doing what it must. The room turns colder

After the last word has left listen for the quiet
rap on the door, for the stranger to wait outside

The Former Jewish District of Hamburg

They sit several rows back in the Kammerspiel
theatre on Hartungstrasse, licks of flame
in hollowed-out eyes, bodies almost visible.
They worked here all those years and left only
for a while, free to return after demolition
crews and landscapers offered a new take
on the Euclidian circle and spokes of camps,
and the archives have given them names the way
heaven is divided into stars each according
to grid, locality, type, constituents, years

The play they have come to see is new. The playbill
tells us it's about our galaxy,
its impossible reach, the many systems with their
black holes, the inexorable pull toward
a ravenous oblivion, the black hole at the centre
that dwarfs them all, unimaginable,
and leaves no witnesses behind

Ida Ehre's direction is flawless, as always,
and she knows the heavens didn't choose any
of the words that shattered like the synagogue's
leaded glass and the other windows, then vanished,
swept away with the ashes, the sky's grey
stretched out like the prayers of those
who don't believe in praying

Ida, at breakfast the lead actor asked you
to read the review aloud while his mother served
eggs and unsalted butter and broke bread
still bakery-warm. She watched you gather crumbs
from the news page, press them into your thumb
and fingertips: *Like words for the stage,*
like eating the words. A connection . . .
and he interrupted you: "the review is mostly
fair to everyone"

Shabbat in Vienna

for Marina and Victor,
and to the memory of Dovid Bergelson

"These stitch marks of recurrence,
like borrowing from others or yourself."
He praises a noun and verb's
exacting force, every stanza a new
and sacred ground sufficient
in itself. The rest, he tells his students,
"is tautological as hell"

or like the images on walls between nations
you and I photographed more than once
in colours of blood, clear bile, blunt bruise —
and the eyes among them following like
informers, found again at the next
sentry tower, sudden as reflux or its burn

or the sandbag nest near the usual
triangular sign at the border crossing,
the machine gun turned on our daughter
because she tried to count petals
of a roadside flower, my wife
marching her fury to the sentry's pit
as he turned his gun away, his arms
and hands pleading our daughter
back into the car because, you said,
innocence can be large as a minefield seeded
with the flowers of paradise

And urgency can wait for hours
at a checkpoint, the first shift of guards
leaving, although they looked our way

as I drafted notes, striking interlined
phrases, writing them again,
working my theme in almost every sentence
like the worm that never sleeps,
the machine gun turned back from the sky
to us when the interrogation began,
endless questions and answers circling
back on themselves, the translator
perspiring words and pauses in the shadow
of the car's open door, not the place
to let on that one of us
understood the repeated back and forth
between them, a language speaking
its purpose

Perhaps you too
would have been reminded
of Russia and stories started there before us
in another language, how one needs to read them
from the beginning, in Yiddish
and translation, see them from the outside,
the world being written,
in order to understand your grandfather's
tales, their doublings, their prodigality
making choices difficult, in the end
joining like scrolls breathing soundlessly

in the ark and a god asleep or far away,
the dog-eared siddur on the floor,
the mutter of dispute around the ark
quieting like the rain, a Shabbat-
ending argument beneath
the balcony's white curve.
And outside the synagogue
armed guards at the shut door
and the Viennese dun of police with Uzis,
two on each corner up and down the street,

the cobblestone glistening, sounds
of boots and shoes and greetings stopped
by two street players' pure
absence of words
miming first our applause and how
easily we lose our footing, then
the world's heaviness, the desperate leaning
into it, white gloves and bent
backs pushing it away again
and again

PAINTING OVER SKETCHES OF ANATOLIA

How to Beat the Heat in Bodrum

When the sun
struts nakedly into the sky
and by mid-morning
its searing indolence is thinking
desert rock

don't imagine stones.
Hold off raising your arms
or chanting orisons.
If you must stare, refrain from staring
with a sky in your gaze.
Remain silent when others rise late
and shout at each other.
Turn your wedding ring
no more than once

Find a breeze if you can.
Let it surround you.
Stay calm. If it means 'maybe'
don't move, let the lizard on the wall
jerk his head up to thrum his throat

You are your own visitor
no need for permission
to be here, to know
how easy it is to stay.
Say the time is not yet;
tonight you will go inside

Olive Harvest on the Terraces

Dirt road below half out of hiding,
and two burros (how like their double
sacks) single-filing to the mill
as if hesitations
in a step will make the way straight,
float an endless roll of hills away
and turn the breeze this way,
silver the orchard trees in fits and starts.

An apparition of white butterflies
veers as one from tree to tree
against the morning's incessant blue.
Where we've stopped under our tree
a lizard, throat pulsing the moment's
desperation, vanishes into the earth.
We're putting down sheets:

today red olives, only one tree.
Raki Mamut, hair black as a coal
seam emblazoned with light, measures
tree and sky and tells me
we won't be long, white *Neyzen*
Yachting shirt ironed smooth,
perfect fit. His wife, Munifer, almond eyes
and dark embroidered dress, cleaning sunglasses
like a pilgrim of the terra incognita within,
in the doorway her mother
bent by osteoporosis to a question mark
no taller than her grandchild
in primary school today. Mamut has never said
marriage to beauty and money although
a dream will divide you, and perhaps
his thinner angular part still knows how to towel
drinking glasses, prop them like bowling pins

in a narrow bar in Turgutreis
at three in the afternoon, small quarrel
of wind redesigning the grass
and palms, the brochures about this place
untrue but his voice in the bamboo hut
bottomless: "the raki is ready,
meine Damen und Herren."

Mamut and I on opposite sides
of the tree, circling as if we're about to invent
revels of ripeness by shaking branches
and listening to the hail-drum of olives.
I stare into the sun, ignite everything,
surprised by the moment it takes for a world
to burn black, yet my jet-lagged
body knows it's time to be here,
as it did north of Tarsus
on the far skirt of the Taurus Range
when the engine chatter of our van stopped
across the road from a man's silhouette
black against morning sun
shooting flames through the harvester —
beyond the harvester golden wheels
of winter wheat and wheels within
the prophet's fiery wheels. And when
these terraces return, first as shimmering
and then as olive trees, Mamut
is halfway to my side, beating languid branches
with a three-metre pole. The rake
Munifer gives me with a Yes/No shake
of her head is smooth in my hands
like skin tingling with details as I climb
the ladder's rungs, strip
the highest branches of leaves
and small pendants blood-brown.

Our second hour of work is losing
method, Mamut and I opening shirts,
pulling them out of our jeans. Truth is,
knowing how much repeats itself,
what is finished or not, what's next,
we want to sit down.
"These trees make you think in ways
you haven't before" — ladder, pole, and rake
the same as last year, and the sacks
and wedding sheets on the ground —
"there aren't that many kinds of olives;
there are many ways to harvest them."

Yes, Mamut, so much of our knowing
comes to nothing, even that
which doesn't lead to bad ends,
and stripping a tree of most of its olives
and many of its leaves is easier
than forgiving our teachers.

"I say a few simple words
and the professor is lost in thoughts,
I like that," Mamut grasping the sheet
by two corners, waiting for me to do the same.
Munifer has been picking leaves and stems
from the litter, unafraid of her body's beauty,
neck and back perfectly straight, cupped hand
sweeping redness back and forth, fingers
alive like a pianist, her face
almost serious as she finally turns back,
rolls a jute sack down as if to step inside,
watches olives roll and mound end to end
across the middle of the sheet,
places the sack at Mamut's edge,
moves it closer, half the open top
underneath, hands and arms
ready.

Far off another olive orchard
with the vagueness of neighbours allowing
something to happen and children's laughter
like the sound of water washing a day's grace
clean at the door.

Ismail's Restaurant

Hair on fire, I leave the lane's narrowness
to an oncoming tractor, turn into Ismail's yard.
His wife smiles sweat beads,
bends down to dip into a pail of
well water, wipes her brow and steps
over a broom to greet me. She can finish
when Ismail returns from the garden, she says,
or when Mustafa comes home from school, but I
help move metal chairs and tables
from the pavingstone patio into the shade
of trees where a brattle of three black hens
loses itself in retreat

Midday has found its hottest hold.
I put fingers and thumbs to my earlobes
until the burn knows something other
than burn and relearns touch independent
of body or chairs, touch belonging wholly
to itself, the sun rubbing dots
of light into the turned earth on the lane's
far side, where furrows give up redness,
root spikes and dry leaves standing on edge
shiny as words from when the time of lemon
and mandarin orchards was over, when Ismail's dream
of a *restoran* kept him awake all night
like summer heat not yet broken

A restaurant has never meant the world to me
or let me fall half-asleep by dawn
or sent my wife to a gourmet cook-off
in Istanbul, but I enjoy liminal evenings
here, spices biding their time, the dome
of stars forming, moths separating
from everything except the heat

of night lanterns. Yet at noon a glass of cold
water that I hold with both hands is enough
for fingers to know themselves as if
for the first time, to know that holding
on does not have to hurt, and for me
to say thank you and my feet feel
the gravel's crushed white perfection
as I return to the lane that takes me
to a wider lane that takes me to the sea

Archaeology in Knidos, 1991

Here archaeology begins
with missing planks on a dock too narrow
for two abreast or a misstep,
for anything more than counting loose boards
under our feet, single-file of purpose
away from the dinghy and the shore
into the past, mainly uphill
on the hard path, our feet
small among mouths
of rodent holes in the brown tobacco earth.
We answer to names with heaving breath —
our captain, my wife with red umbrella,
a young Elena of Hamburg
and, falling behind, you, her Viennese husband,
sourdough amateur archaeologist
with much to go on: new wife,
digs started by others, wine
at sunrise, scorn for your nation's hypocrisies.
Because you pressed the "du"
when my wife and I said "Sie" to the largesse
of eyes behind your raised glass,
you will always stay within sight in this poem.

A past everywhere is a past nowhere,
and so five temples have been found
underfoot, stones mortared by shadows in trenches
marked by signs, misspelled words weathered
like the thorn grass and the path we're told
to follow. Only the Dorian league's
temple to Apollo, somewhere on the far cape
beyond the land bridge, is still in hiding,
rocks and grit settling time as place
inside the promontory round and flat
as a skull before falling steeply to the sea.

"No one is sure," our sandalled captain explaining
in Turkish and German. His yacht is the *Tamas,*
twin in Amharic, like *didymos* on Kos
and the other Greek island we skirted this time,
favouring Euclid's theorem of the hypotenuse,
subtended line stretching in and out
of sea troughs to make our way across
open water in a local storm.
Your Viennese boot scrapes earth
with the self-absorption of a straight razor
through two-day's bristle. You know legends
in which Judas Thomas Didymus, the doubting one,
is the twin of Jesus. Our captain,
nominal Muslim, works his way higher;

his hands order us together
five metres south of the pedestal
Praxiteles' Aphrodite left for a day,
then stepped back up
to her accustomed place with a history
of a new order below — islands, sea lanes, people
old and young, a league of cities, coins
of many kinds, amphorae sweating olive oil
and wine, bronzed sailors sweating their night
with unpainted prostitutes, and gods
who get information firsthand
in small parts, unhappy
with the whole, the future's imperfections.

This dais of a world, more exact
than American archaeologists who found it
almost level, almost a perfect circle,
although shock waves moaning upward
from far beneath the sea brought down
sometimes a roof, sometimes a rush
of powdered air, sometimes a wall
of street-corner interests, or houses

of the dead, their marble-wrought lives
and wreathed after-life littered in weeds.

You agree with our captain, this dais
has lost everything: the Aphrodite in the Louvre
may have come from another place
and time. "When the young began to build the city
a third time, mainly of rubble hauled further back
from the bay, the old saw the goddess
free herself a second time and stride
down to the water's edge, into the sea."
A drowned goddess, more beautiful
in vanishing, more patronized and pampered,
but less audacious than the dais
she deserted.

"A late shoveller," you say; "excavator
of what's left," as you kneel down like a supplicant
forbidden to speak another word, one boot
forward, and then with a wince you pluck
a small coin out of the ground.
A thing of wonder like coins
out of earth or air. As a boy
I counted them, conjured in ones and twos
by my neighbour in blowzy saddleshoes
already unfashionable — from his blond hair
from the evening sky behind me,
always the English Queen's kind face.
But this is Alexander's head,
cupped round in your hand, mostly black
on silver. "It's not Knidan," you tell me,
but it dates from Praxiteles' time. Coins
of this kind are found elsewhere.
A coin, almost perfectly rounded by blood
on its outer edge, settled between life lines
marking off short and long. "The blue glass
we see everywhere underfoot

is Roman; the shards of white and gold
are Greek, or Roman imitations of the Greeks,"
the surf muttering far off in unison
with itself, less precise
than the drop of blood on your boot.

~

Riding sea horses as waves washed the deck,
smacked windows, curled
into the hatchway, drenching our bedding below
had roused night-long regrets
and desire for land. The storm died
abruptly as it had come, like Jesus quieting
the Galilean waters, you said, but the captain
pointed west to where Aeneas lost
his bearings and most of his men.
We helped the captain sweep broken dishes up
before he served a hot breakfast
and your glass of wine,
we looked out to land, and then
we launched a little madness
in a too-small dinghy and came ashore
in two shifts. Earth swayed
underfoot as we worked our way up
to the pedestal, the sun warming our backs,
your wife repeating twice that if there's
a next time she'll bring a small umbrella,
you well to the rear by now,
the breeze filling your sleeves
and greying hair.

~

Here, near the top, where Aphrodite confessed
even she had been mistaken but not deceived,
the wind has ceased. Our backs burn and we turn
away from the dais to face the sun.

Behind and to the left, stern Aegean blue,
before us our yacht in a sea of fire,
and the grey gain and loss of the bay's
long curve in the heat waves and mid-morning mist.

As crickets exchange a few thin notes
the coin has vanished. You've buried it, you say,
where you found it, perhaps a throbbing finger
deeper, another century down,
in a trench you cut with a shard's edge
because the surface layers are hard.

Our captain scrabbles down the shortest way.
The harbour guard beckons the rest of us
with binoculars and white flap of shirt
to his door. He lived five years in Frankfurt
until they scrawled *Türken raus*
on subway cars. He tells us this and asks
that we turn our pockets out to prove
we've gotten nothing from this morning's visit
except his story, too much sun and the deck hand's
call from the dinghy for the women to come first.
But you're the first to leave the post, index finger
bleeding through its wrap like ink
through paper. My wife closes her umbrella
and nods seaward to Elena; you and I
remain on the derelict dock,
inspecting missing parts and sea bottom beneath.
"Tiring climb; I feel older today," your hands
in your pockets. The heat? Our age?
Millennia of obligations uncancelled
although the death of gods discharges them
of theirs? From the laze of ancient stone
and new door the guard watches us, his eyes
unmoving, as if the mind can stop
itself or us. Because
you look back to him and step

into the dinghy a foot from where
the rower marks the floor with three slaps of his hand,
the boat heels and washes our boots
with water it has taken on. We regain balance
by sitting down where we are.
The underworld of sea slides by,
and I know this moment began
in different languages a long time ago
and I'd need to start near the end, explain
how those of our people who stayed
in the Soviet Union aged faster
than those who fled, that those
sent to the Gulag
aged more quickly than the others,
that the women aged first. And whether
we escape or not, we wear only our own shame;
we refuse others'. But after you've waved
to the guard and the dock shrinks
to a thin pencil of grey
I say by the way that gods imprisoned
by worship here must have aged as quickly
as a god self-banished to the bottom of this sea,
and if we visit Knidos again the dock
may be gone.

You, fingering foot
and red sock inside your unlaced boot,
the dinghy heeling into the yacht's shade,
the rower reaching over the water
for the ladder, and I see
what he can't: between bloody-smirch
of your finger-wrap and second finger,
the silver and black of the coin
summoning out.

Entering Cappadocia

Villages riding at anchor in the fog,
minarets pondering distance
silence, all the signs
you followed driving
here that led to rolls
of time before time unscrolling
valleys of tufa cones
and chimneys half-hiding
other valleys, lawless geometry
from when the world
was on fire, honeycombed
stone tents and crags
that make this high precipice
where you stand at the sheer drop
unremarkable, glorious
as light pours over you

The Medusa of Didyma

The way I said *No,*
scent of jasmine
and almond blossom
still strong in my hair

No longer drunk priests and
heroes of our city grasping
my breasts and invoking
gods and my shame.
Afraid as I am, my mouth devours
their seasons, every leaf,
petiole and stem, a destiny
only young mortals find unusual,
yet no more terrible
than turning ordinary gods
great and small
and creatures
that sleeplessness imagines
into quarried rock, every god
polished marble now,
every creature perfect

even my heart's priestess,
hair alive like mine,
wild as a nest of vipers moving
as one, who loved me,
whose screams felt betrayal
in so many things —
those nearest looking the other way
arm across face to shrines
of small-roofed prayers —
her final prophecy abjured

when she refused the slope's
temple litter in the overgrowth
for a museum's virginal white
where others approach only
so far, no closer

Sister.
O sister . . .

Ancient Dwelling Below the Black Sea

for Harun and the marine archaeological team

Grandfather stared this way
from the far side, Crimea,
while others slept as though
the future could find this shore at the end
of the water's moonlit road
without foundering,
the sand no longer firm underfoot

So much to trust in order to live
our every-day without sinking
through the world. Yes,
Tomas Tranströmer,
almost too much for you,
and for me when sudden rollers
return that in a lake of icebergs laid
the canoe on its side,
the hard slice of water, how under water
I tried to call my friend,
how one can hold breath almost forever,
how self-reproach enters first
at the nose, then the mouth, how stones
much larger than houses can rise
from the blackness to bear us up
the last half mile

It's a question of what one feels,
if anything, and the simple elegance
of your Swedish, calm as the sea with words
of trust, some of them unbearable

If you were to dive forty metres
down with me to the broad ledge,

rasps of breath rushing upward
like a lifeline of light as the impossible
dark gathered beneath us,
the chill would be at least as great
as an iceberg lake, pressure
tingling our numbness, feet not feeling
amphorae and the broken cornice stone

I waiting to leave, to rise with you

If it came to this,
your watchfulness no doubt
would hold back from the drop-away
beyond the edge, the canyon
that deadens by degrees,
everything down there unchanged,
wrecks, anchors, cargo, millennia,
even our bodies, cleaner, more perfect
than the clay jar you reach for,
whose meaning, almost whole, you mull,
how waters of the Golden Horn
and Marmara Sea warmed by summer's
eternities once held themselves
back behind a Bosporus
awash with trade, choosing hours
and sounds of what might be, the future
trembling with everything else
when the scarp's bulwark shifted yet
another inch or so toward us

Midday Meal at the Tigris River

It seemed we had let something break
through the day's slow stammers to seize us
as though we had risked being there,
the kingfisher preening an olive tree's
braids of wind-silvered green as we entered
the cave, our words few as we stepped
further back beyond the red ash

Her eyes flickered a moment of white before
she speared fish from the pan and one-handed
blue plates across the glare
of the cave's mouth and the light at the river's
margin, a motion ready for glory,
the glory of the body's joy
inside a cliff by the Tigris,
our shoes sun-blind outside
with everything else, you and I
on burgundy carpets and camel saddles
draped in burgundy cotton and silk,
eating small fish, crisped
fins and all, finger food,
moments settling themselves
with the ash, the warmth inside us
taking its time like the blood's pulse
in the veins

                    rising with us to usher
charcoal- and grease-blackened
plates to a small rack the woman pointed out
because I hadn't noticed, my eyes
sorting instead from the dimness
a skitter of maybe between your bare feet

There are people who eat scorpions whole,
long crescent tail, anus, stinger, prosoma,
and pedipalp, but a scorpion's body parts
can also find direction for its many legs
to best the carpet's upturned border
and pitch into the dark where a cave
becomes more than itself

like the Tigris, broad and full as the infinite
it gathers from all the claims upon it,
words added without end.
And your 'O' little more than a breath
and less than a word teetering toward
the light

Morning Prayer

for my grandson, Daniel Kerem Bozkurt

Child as much as grandfather,
I put on yesterday's clothes
and something else I've wakened to,
follow where my grandson goes,
through the high Ottoman foyer, out
the double door, only a step behind
his Turkish "come," past
the orchard keeper's cottage of stone walls,
small windows, red-tiled roof and open
door. Daniel calls out "Mister
brother" to Ali, who yesterday
picked at knots with his teeth, all the while
humming through his nose like a muted violin,
a child's song, the same melody as in English,
mouth pulling one way and the other, in turn,
humming with all his strength.
And then my grandson twisting and lurching
on Ali's lap as they rode the puny, raucous,
doorless three-wheeled truck
heads down as one
between trees in rows: mandarin,
lemon, grapefruit and lime
green as the hearts Daniel crayoned
last evening and the one
with a spear in it red as a pomegranate

I knew he'd be at the bed this morning,
elfin arm tapping my pillow stuffed
with dreams. We walk to where Ali
is watering saplings on the far side,
where Daniel may not have been before
but now, mired in water and mud,

reaches for my hand. The splash of the hose
like his laughter in hiding

Repertoire of hunger chirring in the weeds,
a hunger anyone can understand,
familiar as the call for breakfast.
The muezzin's invocation to prayer
begins, swelling on the wind that wishes itself
landward, searches dappled light
in this valley of orchards and sky-high
arbor vitae. And the day's cause that
winkered my wakening an hour ago
before folding away is near again,
an old habit like the muezzin's cry,
this child of my blood and I
summoned,
passing in and out of shadows

Hand-Painted Plates of Nicæa

Endless orchard green to our right,
on our left cat's-paw shadows pivoting on the lake,
hurrying to keep us company to Iznik
as though to bid us welcome (*Hosh geldinis*).
Ahmed, our driver, offers the Greek word
for Nicæa like forbidden fruit. So this is where
centuries of strange desire were plotted?
Alexander's gleaming, double-edged
imagination, Pliny's high-end Roman gossip,
yet another earthquake, stronger than the last,
sending do-nothing gods packing, mornings
and evenings now passing through the gates
of Hadrian's new, heaven-inspired city walls.
A Byzantine emperor's ultimatum
to his feuding council of bishops, the first draft
of a creed opened and cut apart like the marbled hills
of Anatolia or the votes of the Arians,
and the cross and sword became one,
like a triune god. The earth heaved again,
and again, but city walls and churches returned
to their importunity of place stone by stone,
the Aya Sofya larger each time, seeking room
for a cruciform until Orhan drew a circle
around the walls that stilled the city
and its appetites, and Tamerlane changed
the day's and night's routines
and Nicæa's name to Iznik.

Above the cobbled streets Mongol gutturals
and lisps from the upper floor shed the night's
emptiness, giving way at the city's edge
to the pitched Farsi of craftsmen from Selim's
new empire transported here,

their Persian songs of banishment bleeding
the Iznik red,
which my wife and I
admire in the most expensive plates. We buy
one and two traditional Ottoman,
a trinity of colours wrapped with care
for explanation to customs officers.

But those half-starved Persian artists
exiled by horsemen on the world's four winds,
held back only by the bottomless gulf
the living cannot cross, corpses stacked
neatly as firewood on either side. Those
who escaped unlearned heaven and hell,
and those who didn't had time enough
to say farewell to friends still at home, polite
as always, like the villagers Father left behind,
who bade the secret police welcome,
stepped aside, and no one, not even the police,
knew where in the Gulag the men would be sent
and who might return.

Orchard floors
clean of grass and weeds have been harrowed
dark as the lake. We can smell the earth,
we can hear bees frantic with the last blossoms
of the season. On the orchard roads blue tractors
are followed by a swirl of feathered radiance.

Tomorrow we fly back to Bodrum's
cobblestone drives, off-white marble walks
and the turquoise bay of Bitez. *Come, we're home,*
the wide gate open to what's between us
and house, Selim, our son-in-law, kissing us
on both cheeks, a mourning dove's
single-note reviewing yesterday, a child

running toward us from the orchard, past
the massive 500-year-deep furrows
of an olive tree as we step through the shadow
of the Ottoman mansion and into the foyer,
the far glass wall opening to the atrium with its sea-
encrusted amphorae on their sides, held close
by trees.

The white of the near wall measures
the distance of an empire and hand-painted
plates of heaven's native Persian blue,
earth's talismanic green, and
Iznik red.

Painting with Reds in Eastern Turkey

1

Arm raised like a holy man's.
He's ugly, toothless,
eats scraps left outside for homeless
dogs, Antiochan prostitute
in crimson and gold, crimson for his lust
and gold for his love of it.
Where he lives, unknown,
but people from Aleppo remember.
Given a meal he'll sleep at your door
for a day in his carmine wool cap.

2

Ancient stone stairs rising through narrow
possibilities, run-off channel holding roots
of the alleyway like railway ties, yellow light
leaking in. In Van the last turn balances
you and the rose-stone house, perfect Ottoman
square against layered ferrous cliffs,
this fire-red almost enough
for torn ribbons of vermilion sky
set adrift over the Caucasus and a curtain
of rain lowering onto Ararat.

3

All the lands and people he had made his own
and his father, Terah, buried here
only weeks ago were not enough to keep
Abraham in Harran. But no return
to Mesopotamia. That would loosen
the knit in him. Townspeople
gathered to accept his unfrayed
mats and tribal carpets, even his pots
and amphorae, and neighbours waited to drink
the last of his sugared wine. Outside
the door he considered the large brown amphora's
wide mouth, pieces broken away
like loyalties. *It will stay,*
and he cupped the water with his right hand,
let it fall through the other hand and blacken
the dust. What to do? But he knew.

Our footprints in the light rain are stopped
by the patience of a lamb tight-tethered
at Harran's third mud-brick beehive house,
the large cerise X whitening more
than the lamb's small-ridged back,
no hay, only water (the Bayram festival
tomorrow), and just outside the polished
clay threshold a woman's small rubiate
shoes pointing in from yesterday
This is where I've always lived.

4

Your clothes are not scarlet
as these, yet you fancy them as five shirts,
one dress and four *shalvar* pants
wide as the morning
and pulled one at a time out of
rinse water Sedona-red, pinned
to a line linking margins, single shape
of cut-outs bellying down
from the lavender door post and up to
the sun-glazed tiles of a terracotta
roof opposite, above the window's
bakery pyramids of naked bread
looking out.

5

Minotaur Brit, old at thirty-something,
shorts small as his beefcake
companion's topless blush of bikini —
skin dark, an Italian cello's glow
but white creases unfolding
accordion-like as they walk the shore
outside Adana, everywhere
left to go, the sand's glitter
working on a thought far ahead.

6

Father Gabriel's monastery kept holy
by gentleness, black caftan
and burnt sienna slippers,
and by sleeping only a few hours,
drinking bitter tea, paying attention
to visitors, never forgetting some of them
may be spirits, like demons that came
one evening as black dogs. Otherwise
there would be more dogs,
and at night birds
with the devil's cinnabar eyes.

7

Ah, Mustafa Kemal. What young soldiers
will kill and die for by tens
of thousands. Imagine. Telling others
drinking with you like Manet's café crowd
(although you usually drank alone,
drained of patience to the mark
on the bottom) that you, Atatürk,
would die young but not your new
republic, the flag everywhere,
heraldic red snapping west to east
in the unremitting wind.

The traveller in Mardin paints school girls
in tartan claret and blue, above them
sky unfurled, the flag unsure.

Traditions and the New Near Mardin

Roads are modern here until they stop,
defer without argument to cart
tracks or narrow rock-bruised paths
used by boys breathing songs the elders
taught them to sing while calling
sheep or goats, the past storied and sung.
All stanzas by heart, the wisdom keepers
say, as many as the words remember.

And here I am, sitting at ease on the edge
of Mesopotamia, a warm evening's
confidence in reconstructed legs
after hours of walking the hills as though
this were my land in another life or a place
I could make for myself. There — Syria,
and more to the north the Tigris, and then Kurdish
Iraq. The eagle overhead has stopped his screams,
and there's no need for signs of more agreement.
Too many searches have meant loneliness,
or seeking friends in the future, or searching for
my place when I'm already there — what's here
and what's imagined sitting with locked arms
as a world's silence dreams, the presence strange
yet familiar as a voice recorded, my voice,
on how the pastoral's harmonies and light
and stones of sharp misgivings come to be.

~

Prior to sun, moon, stars and hematic
glyphs what the gods know within
themselves is twilight unreckonable
and the magic of pure mind.
That's why Nin-kasi, daughter of Ninti,

sings her creation story as warning against
the old mathematics that starts things ahead
of themselves to keep them as they are,
like hanging a wondrous garden by
a river before a world is made,
a garden more perfect than the crystalline
springs and the blue of a sacred lake
she knows will come in their own time.

The white gleam of new construction
stitching sky to the amphitheatre
of morning hills. Treeless.
Their goat paths breathing hard
down to where a herd huddles against
the infinite privacy of the plains.

"Five kilometres from Mardin
on the hill by the forever Plain
is found the Mesopotamia Resort.
Hotel that combines the tradition with
modern and provides all services
that requires the modern way of life."

Lyre-like whispers water gardens
hanging from the nothing, gardens
so set apart that women and children,
cattle, rainbows, Sumerian leavened
light breaking through, perfume
of the little-leaf Linden and green
shores unwinding themselves downstream
are not allowed inside the gate
guarded by heaven's bated breath.

Two goats crowded at the cliff's edge
slip, plunge star-like, shadowed blur
soundless with the world's weight
written in the air. Birds without wings.

"In the Swimming pool bar and in
the Main bar you may enjoy
your drink. There are also available Mini
Market, Fitness Centre, Jacuzzi,
and Children's Playground," a surplus
offered for the moment like a church
in Quebec City, buyer's bargain
since the playground is included
as long as what you see
on the outside of the church
remains the same until the inside
stops changing, which is like tradition
and the modern when the curve
of the pastoral crosses itself and the two
tangents to the curve coincide.

Nin-kasi tells of a scribe with whey-skinned
brow and mascaraed eyes, beautiful
as her mother. No task ever finished,
he'd bite his tongue hard as he
imagined tablets and amphorae,
and Nin-kasi seeded the grey of his hooded
world with indecisive jars,
a grain head's fatness, yeasty
ripeness of dew and rain, and helped
him forget them for a thousand
dim-lit years humming
of creation coming quiet as wind,
breath after breath before he
remembered an amphora's shape,
lifted its weightlessness against
the heavens, the few degrees above
the horizontal enough to figure
its height, a cubit and a hand.

The herd is a line drifting up toward
the last light between the sky and plain.

The rooftop restaurant offers
a night of ghost-light flickers
from Syria pointing to nothing visible.
"Tonight's specials: lazanya and salad.
Chay or first beer free."
In the main bar mixed drinks pale
as a week-old rose in a water
bowl and men watching each others'
cell phone pleas and overweight
courage of words shielding them
in their back and forth.

The scribe cried gently out
at the way endless seas and land
began to swim into view together
with a surge like a river welling to water
the face of the earth and the simple garden
near a bank of clay, clay smooth
as honey and dates and the slim-ankled
woman with flowing hair and arms
beckoning him to walk with her
along the river. He ran toward her
to ask the word for woman and how
things happen as they do and why,
and whether she also was two-
thirds mortal and one-third
god. No more memorized records
of the gods' caprices. On the bank
he would let her watch as he drew
a stylus from his breast, tested
its point with index finger, turned
it about, half closed his eyes
and began a song in the clay: 'now
a river goes out from the land to water
the garden. From there it divides and divides
again . . .'

Moonlight flows like a river in the plain.
The bell of the lead goat far out of sight
tinkles as though whatever it is has started.

~

One idea of this place is silence,
another its contradictions. The goats will have
lain down for the night. When they are driven
to more distant pastures, the hotel will be
updated and reopen under new owners,
and the road's obsessions with the lip of hills
will push on to a new end. The scribe's
descendants will be taken as booty to where
a garden once was hung, and there they'll
rewrite creation although the records
disagree and much memory
has gone to sleep like the goats on the far slopes
of this hill and some like the goats that fell.
There is glory in this, and wandering doubt
before but rarely after, great as the glory
of a five-year-old in Bitez on the Aegean
following his fingers through his first piano
recital.

Listen, friend, foot-wrenching
paths and two hundred miles of plain
will forget a new hotel, artless imitations
of modernity, two dead goats
and me, my scrapes of curiosity,
wayfare notes, the small excitement when
Nin-kasi tried to steal the day away.
But evening printed my shadow on
a stone, and after that the night had
nowhere else to turn, its perfection
truer than any I, a traveller stopped
by nightfall at this plain, could have conjured
or striven for.

Expatriate

Today the regional wind-surf races,
curved backs careening past
full sails and brown-knotted bodies
and through the Aegean's turquoise tension
of swells and gravity, boards on edge,
a hide-and-seek of rainbow rooster tails
across the afternoon

Tomorrow will follow yesterday, fill
the amphitheatre of sea with light and first-time
wind-surfers arguing sails out of the water,
frog-legging themselves back
onto the board, talking the body into position,
letting the sail find the wind, heeling
over, falling forward this time.
Endless chances to right themselves,
catch the wind in a perfect broad reach
without knowing it, swoosh past
splayed bikinis and boards to people watching
from the marina's choir of piers, wave
to them, come about like a veteran,
the body's joy bent into its simplest form,
a fishmonger on the largest dock
shouting his approval as he slits fish bellies
gill to tail, thumbs out the guts
in a single stroke

You've come to Lycia many times, flushed new words
out of hiding, let them break through
stammers of repetition and fold into
your said and unsaid life. You've stayed hours
at the shore's dalliance below the All Season
Restaurant's white tables and blue umbrellas,
arthritic knees clicking whatever season

has come to stay again in walls, gardens,
the sea. You want what you have,
but you review today's races the way
you replayed baseball games as a boy,
finding ways to win, to cancel errors.
And you wonder about yesterday's reason
for standing with hands on the chair's back,
the chair the head waiter brought you,
why you said "not today, but thank you
very much" to his offer of *chay* or Turkish coffee
on the house, your eyes and few words
softening any failure. You can't explain
why you've extended your stay a second time,
why you half-expect someone whose name
has escaped you again to notice you
and not the sunset's runaway red, step off
the boardwalk and across the sand's
sleeves of light, kiss both your cheeks,
the first cheek a second time, sit down
on the empty chair, lean back
with a voice one uses when there will be
no others, and ask how you are,
both of you looking out to sea

Namaz at Dawn

The notebook new, empty except for
I wonder how it will be without poetry and then
without words. This is the time a notebook
leaves me here, alone, the time stars grow small
and night is taken away over the high ridge
that loses its edge to light breathing past
a silhouette of windmills and watchtower ruins.
My feet feel the full length of all-night bars,
coffee houses, unlit balconies and the sea's
meniscus of lines in the sand where stray dogs
stretch away the hurt of the boardwalk's
laddered dark and the deeper dark of boards
removed for paving stones stacked like amphorae
to replace them. A dragonfly's

filigree of wings turns transparent
in a slipstream of light. In and out
of time, between water and a yacht's
rise and fall steady as an anchored
heart. Along the public pier small rings
grow large where fish nosed up a moment ago
to feed, where a man inside his towel
walks head down to the far end as though
to absorb the immensity of the muezzin's
amen and a donkey's morning desires
echoing far into the hush. The bather
enters a half-halo of water, divides it like a seal,
changes course to find the sun

and I find the key's brass bulk
in my pocket. I know where home is.
Step around a dog. Nod to the woman
leaving the bakery, a loaf in each hand,
her shoulder bag empty. Put away

my notebook's false start and aftermath
of empty pages. No need
to turn them over and over, to fill vacancy
with what might have been, to say that day
is here and needs an answer lest
it mingle like Bitez with our lives
or with the impatience of infants wakened
by the muezzin and the donkey, fretting
one at a time and then in chorus

There is much that will not change today —
the day's warm drift like the coming and going
of tourists, the journalist at the Shah Hotel
who put down fork and knife last evening
to say that Torontonians are not at all like Turks,
the main street's name that means heaven's door,
construction workers sipping morning *chay*
through toothbrush mustache
black as missing teeth

or the small snake
that lives in the stone wall next door
and does no harm to anyone.
May it live for a thousand years

THINK OF THIS EARTH, MY LOVE

The Pastoral

Find an innocence naked and garish
as a child's orchard book on an oak floor,
every page an unpruned tree,
the child on knees, the trees yielding to page-
turning fury, caulicles letting go,
the many ripe and unripe fruits
falling to the earth, bruises blackening
until the litter is what remains

But save one fruit, the kind that sets
a child's teeth on edge, let it ripen,
let its fragrance ride the air, first taste
like an ache that stays, coaxing the tongue's
need for softness, the blue-eyed child
leaning forward, reaching to turn the page

The Season That Ages Words

i

An angel is the hope of a message
larger than itself if we believe
the white circle in which it stands,
its English eyes, its pale hand smaller
than most but otherwise perfect

Forgive me for writing this season
and memory. Winter is long enough
as it is. In the golden nightlights
near the Plaza the street
shines with salt and snow
and small drifts clumsy with the quiet
white of hospitals feel
the world crawl one way,
then another, around them

ii

In the beginning the word said
"let there be winter"
but already the woman had felt change
in the air and the reserve of warmth
within, and she covered the man
with her thin blue coat.
On the Plaza's south side the flowers
were brown, and by afternoon
black trees jutted out of snow,
the sky between them immense
with two red-tailed hawks
circling lower, one screaming
its ice-age secret over
and over to the river below

iii

For all the students in the doorway
and their long disorder of laughter on the
channel's far side the wind
has made its adjustments,
and the man watching them
from the bench by the river-walk
subsides into what remains of him

iv

Winter read out of itself.
How none of the shadows is right.
How the hawk will not relent.
How students have come outside to argue.
How the stillness of new ice at the edge
explodes like a rifle shot. How
the woman buying a newspaper
is warmed by the setting sun

Winter Solstice

These leaves underfoot
frozen, your boots breaking them
with the vagueness of thin glass
on the front walk, grass, the orchard
slope, each step into the night cold nerves
of contact, the numb outer skin
a kind of permission to wonder what
to walk through or where to stop
and look into the dark edge of
a galaxy's swirl large enough to choose
between loneness and belonging,
the wind lightly cuffing your ears
like a mother reaching out beyond
her anger, so simple, so meticulous,
and someone else walking within you
watching you step by short step
back toward the open door
amazed, the footprints next to him
each for a moment ablaze
with moonlight

Spring Song, March

Think of this earth, my love.
Notice the garden's brow
furrowed from the inside out,
a dead ground squirrel at the ivy's
ragged edge, jay feathers here
on the moss under the plum tree's
bare details, around our hands
and knees imperfect circles
of artillery weed ready to catapult
white seeds in wider circles,
winter's wreckage of leaves
ridged along the large patch
of rock daphne bursting out first
blossoms of immodest pink,
and everywhere between the trees
and rock ledge spears pushing
their secrets up like memory's

pale surprise of green. A garden
can fold light and the thinking heart
into itself, and sometimes the future
is discernible in our hands and face,
reminding us of last fall's designs,
how some things work out well, even
in this year of winter kill, and the new life
we find on our knees

Spring Song, April

If you have to wait for a long time,
you have to seize hold of the waiting.
— Peter Hoeg, *Smilla's Sense of Snow*

If you've seen enough the world may
repeat itself all night,
the dark grown beautiful
as Raphael's child angels.
Between the clock's soundless snap
of hands and your wife's nakedness
formed perfectly for sleep and the boundaries
of her next vast dream
the moon struts even higher and the firs
grow taller, their fierce attention darker
as you watch them draw back
into the hills,
the hills into the mountains,
mountains into the phantasmal dark's
brief wait until the sky's edge
strains into light, heaves
itself over the mountains'
daze of peaks, through a flash
of trees, through the burst
of upward blossoming boughs,
through the glass door's dust-map
of elsewhere
squared upon the floor,
coming and going,
waiting for the sun to figure
its way through silence
one small cloud at a time

Juan de Fuca Evensong

Small dome of a seal's periscope
and gulls rising and falling
in the fresh-wrapped sound
of water near the black pier,
the sound that draws you to
what's there: the sun red
and bloated on an ocean.
You think endless chambers as it bleeds
slowly down, its pulsing emptiness
reaching toward you like a great hand
with a hundred crimson fingers and
a small cry somewhere between
the calm riding the dark
and the wave breaking against
the table rock on which you stand.
Your sandalled feet chart your bearing
as the foghorn hoots long enough
to surprise you and bend the shore's
lifeline of phosphorescent foam

You let the wind's suddenness
of nowhere slip away only to find you
still here on the rock, the night's canopy
open for stars, mountain silhouettes,
the water's restlessness.
You want them all

including the dark, its longing
for this world that waits to be emptied,
filled, waits for you to find
each of the ten or twelve steps
down the lee side of the rock
backward into the night, fingers

like tactile hair, the search and hold
never the same, legs of muscle, ridged bone
and titanium borrowing certainty
from the step just found

as you wait, almost down,
wearing the night like dew

Daybreak in the Kootenays

The sky's blue full as lungs with the morning's
chill, light between the peaks
drawing up by inches, and a moment
of separation — forest, highway, cars
and the sound of a horn from the ungainly
earth-down limp of what could be
a bear loosely held together.
It's a young cow moose
rising from the swale this side
the road, its accord
with direction plain enough
although the breeze slams the door
of our cabin

Later I try to tell others
how certainty moved without interruption,
how her hoofs moved stones
in the grass, how her nose nuzzle
felt against my shoulder,
the nubs of her head against my ribs
and arm. Their moss-like velvet,
the slowness of her stare, and yes,
her belly's breathing as she lay
down at my feet. Something
drawn across her gaze had passed
between us in those breaths,
in that lying down —
the concentrated stillness of the soul,
the morning of a world
taken in, given back

Raccoons After Dark

The sky burns away
as a chickadee in the orchard
undoes itself with small-talk repetitions,
stopping, as if to come close

like the ground cover underfoot.
There are evenings when the body's aches
rehearse what it's taken all day
to understand, that the earth can claim me
as a tree no longer visible
can claim a bird on a slip of branch,
and I can say to the dark
I'll finish raking tomorrow, but I'm
still where I belong, glorious decay
slow to growth and anger
like the Mirabelle tree's lichens
that cannot reach beyond themselves
and therefore give way
to plums yellow with a brush of red
enough for a long day's foreground,
and now, at this moment,
for eyes walking their small fierce fire
up into the randomness of night
like stars

Walking the Harbour

Drift nets and purse seines
no longer stacked on the piers
like well-rounded narratives,
one laid out beginning to end
as though to prove largesse is nothing
but pure reception, and three nets
coiled unevenly on the street
below Slav Hill: "Free. Please help
yourself." This village casts wide nets
and even if its mornings are too large
and loose to hold much of what passes
through, walking the harbour is about
getting somewhere, where you are,
no matter if the fishing boats
are home or throttling circles far
north in currents off the evergreen-
sharp Alaskan coast

The clouds' drift-down makes the best
of what the edgy slope
of Swede Hill is giving it, and your desire,
gentled by the rain that started without
your notice, pledges belonging
although the fleet left days ago
with the priest's first and second blessing,
all the berths empty as shrines
except for the seal's dome of eyes and mouth
turned this way. Your feet guided you
here without once counting the steps

A cormorant folds into the black of its wings.
Nothing is lost

What the Fraser Valley Left Unsaid

The end of Canada reached long ago
following the sun's urgency to the Pacific.
Anxious settlers and those
who lent us credit heard about
the end of history,
which came quickly, no chance to prepare,
but smaller, frugal times remained
like consolation,
and we gave up dreams
for the heart's ordinary pulse

Each year our bodies more real
like words twisted free of us
in the evening tall as Lombardy poplars
planted in rows by ancestors,
the land drained and surveyed,
a first house framed and shingled,
then another, a road over Majuba Hill
above the smoke streaming eastward from fields
of burning stumps and brush

The air is clear now, the heart's hunger firm
as salmonberries where stones hear water
breathing closer, coming hard
in more than one direction.
Feet at many purposes find
the other shore where ferns unfurl
their small wetness
and Douglas firs give themselves
to what is there

As for the children, we know where they
can be found, their times of joy,
and we are asking permission
to go there, to let them know
that others may come

One day I will offer our children this poem
as love letter, ears ringing with pressure
from the other side of time. When ears
ring like this they hurt enough
to annul our love of place and the last
thing we hoped to describe
to the end.
Yet it's not the same for everyone.
For some the sky will tilt firmly
above the trees
to the steady blue
of mountains where the valley ends

Notes

"Margaret Fuller Returns to New York"

Epigraph is from *American Heritage Magazine*, Vol, 8, issue 2.

"Pierre Loti"

Assumed name of Julian Viaud (1850-1923), Romantic French novelist, travel writer, memoirist, naval officer and adventurer. At the beginning of his writing career he lived briefly in Istanbul, and he later revisited the city. He was much admired in Turkey for his support of the Turkish war of independence.

"Shabbat in Vienna"

Dovid Bergelson (1884-1952): Grandfather of Marina Raskin, he was one of Russia's two greatest Yiddish prose writers (Isaac Bashevis Singer is the better-known of the two). Bergelson was executed on his birthday on Stalin's order.

Synagogue in Vienna: Der Stadttempel, which was attacked in 1981 by Palestinian terrorists with machine guns and hand grenades.

"How to Beat the Heat in Bodrum"

Bodrum, a major resort city on the Gulf of Gökova in southwestern Turkey, is the former Halikarnassos.

"Archaeology in Knidos, 1991"

Dorian league: The reference here is specifically to six Dorian cities in Asia Minor, including Knidos and Halikarnassos. These cities were part of a Dorian alliance in Asia Minor, Greece and Crete that by the fifth-century BCE rivalled Persian power as well as the Ionian cities of Asia Minor and Greece.

Kos: Greek island not far from Bodrum; thus the Greek spelling "didymos."

Praxiteles' Aphrodite left for a day: One legend has the statue vanishing briefly, then returning to her dais and rightful role.

Türken raus: Anti-Jewish graffiti in Nazi Germany, with Turks now substituted for Jews.

"The Medusa of Didyma"

Medusa images, while common in Greece and Turkey, are not identical, and there are variations in the Medusa myth.

"Hand-Painted Plates of Nicæa"

A Byzantine emperor's ultimatum...like a triune god: Emperor Constantine's conclave in 325 CE to hammer out basic orthodox Christian doctrines and policies on behalf of a civil religion for his empire.

Bitez: A town some 10 kilometres west of Bodrum.

"Painting with Reds in Eastern Turkey"

Van (canto 2): A major city and region in northeastern Turkey on the trade route with Iran and not far from the Caucasus mountain range. Once home to a substantial Armenian population.

Bayram (canto 3): Kurban Bayrami, traditionally a festival when lamb, sheep, goat or cow is slaughtered and much of the meat given to the poor.

Atatürk (canto 7): "Father of the Turks." The name was assumed by Mustafa Kemal, brilliant general and founder of the modern Turkish Republic.

"Traditions and the New Near Mardin"

Nin-kasi: An ancient Sumerian goddess born of pristine fresh water. Like her mother, Ninti, she was associated with underground aquifers, lakes, streams, springs and the like. She was credited with creating beer and introducing it to humankind.

"Expatriate"

Lycia: A region in southwestern Turkey in the provinces of Antalya and Muğla.

"Namaz at Dawn"

Namaz: Turkish word for *Azan,* the Muslim call to prayer.

About The Author

Author, editor or co-editor of seventeen books, Leonard Neufeldt was born and raised in the immigrant Dutch-Russian Mennonite hamlet of Yarrow, BC. His grandfather and father, placed under arrest by Bolshevik agents for transport to the Gulag, escaped to Canada via Spain, Cuba and Mexico. Neufeldt graduated summa cum laude from Waterloo Lutheran University (Wilfred Laurier) and received his MA and PhD in the USA. He and his wife have spent most of their professional years in America and abroad, notably in Europe and Turkey. Lecture tours have taken him to India, Germany, Korea and China. Over the years he has been the recipient of numerous awards for his scholarship as well as poetry.

Eco-Audit
Printing this book using Rolland Opaque 30 instead of virgin fibres paper saved the following resources:

Solid Waste	Water	Air Emissions
20 kg	1,611 L	181 kg